IMMIGRANTS
FROM
SOMALIA
AND
OTHER AFRICAN COUNTRIES

BY JESSICA GUNDERSON

CONSULTANT:
MIRIAM E. DOWNEY, MLS
CHILDREN'S LIBRARIAN
IMMIGRATION EQUALITY ADVOCATE

CAPSTONE PRESS
a capstone imprint

Fact Finders Books are published by Capstone Press,

1710 Roe Crest Drive, North Mankato, Minnesota 56003

www.mycapstone.com

Library of Congress Cataloging-in-Publication data is available on the Library of Congress website.

978-1-5435-1381-3 (library binding)

978-1-5435-1385-1 (paperback)

978-1-5435-1391-2 (ebook PDF)

Summary: Gives an overview of the modern immigrant experience in today's uncertain world, including why they left their home country and what they're seeking in the United States. Easy-to-understand language and dynamic graphics help explain this often contentious issue that's a hot topic in today's media.

Editorial Credits

Editor: Jennifer Huston

Production Artist: Kazuko Collins

Designer: Russell Griesmer

Media Researcher: Eric Gohl

Production specialist: Laura Manthe

Photo Credits: AP Photo: Nasser Nasser, 9; Getty Images: Joe Alexander, 7, Melanie Stetson Freeman, 19, Portland Press Herald, 17, 18, Scott Peterson, 14, Stringer/Mohamed Abdiwahab, 15, The Washington Post, 21, Tom Williams, 23, Universal Images Group, 4; iStockphoto: PeterHermesFurian, 11; Newscom: Polaris/John Rudoff, 16, UPI/Madeline Marshall, 22, ZUMA Press/Ardavan Roozbeh, 25, ZUMA Press/Carlos Gonzalez, 28, ZUMA Press/Glen Stubbe, 29; Shutterstock: bioraven, throughout (passport stamps background), demidoff, cover, dikobraziy, cover (background), 1, Nasi_lemak, 27, Sadik Gulec, 13

Design Elements: Shutterstock

Source Notes:

p. 26: Somalis in Minnesota Oral History Project, Oral History Interviews of the Somalis in Minnesota Oral History Project. Minnesota Historical Society. Oral history interview with Deq Ahmed, August 31, 2014.

Printed in the United States of America.
PA021

TABLE OF CONTENTS

WHY IMMIGRANTS LEAVE THEIR HOMES

Before the Pilgrims arrived in 1620, only American Indians lived in what is now the United States. Since then, the United States has become a nation of **immigrants**. Leaving your home country to live somewhere else can be scary. You'd have to leave behind your friends, your school, and your home. You might not know the language or the customs of your new country. These are the challenges immigrants face every day.

Because of **drought**, food and water are very scarce in parts of Africa. This leads many people to move to other countries. In this image, people in Ethiopia have lined up to fill jugs with water.

Since the late 1960s there has been an upward swing in immigrants from Africa living in the United States. Africa is home to more than 50 countries with many cultures, languages, and religions. Throughout the continent, the landscape ranges from deserts to tropical rain forests. Changing weather patterns and drought have caused the deserts to increase in size. This has led to a lack of water and food shortages for many Africans.

NUMBER OF AFRICAN IMMIGRANTS LIVING IN THE UNITED STATES BY DECADE

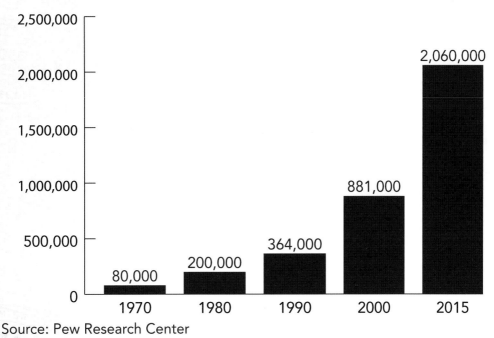

Source: Pew Research Center

immigrant—someone who comes from one country to live permanently in another country
drought—a long period of weather with little or no rainfall

African immigrants come to the United States for higher education or career opportunities. Many Africans also leave their homes due to **famine**, poverty, and war. The 1990s saw an increase in **refugees** from Rwanda and Somalia due to **civil wars**. More recently, unrest in Sudan has led many people to flee their home country.

THE HISTORY OF AFRICANS IN AMERICA

The first Africans in America did not come here by choice. Between the 15th and 19th centuries, an estimated 12 million Africans were forced into slavery. More than 10 million of them came to the Americas. The voyage across the Atlantic Ocean was long, the ships were crowded, and many people died.

The enslaved Africans tried to maintain their **culture**. However, most slaveowners would not allow them to speak their native language or practice their religion. In 1808 the U.S. government made it illegal to bring anyone into the country to be sold as a slave. However, slavery continued in the United States until 1865.

In the late 19th century, the United States began setting limits on immigrants based on their race or country of origin. Later, the Immigration Act of 1924 limited the number of immigrants from Africa to just 1,100 per year. In 1965 the Immigration and Nationality Act got rid of limits based on race. Since then the number of African immigrants has been steadily rising.

Millions of people from Ethiopia were affected by severe droughts and famine in the mid-1980s, including this mother and child.

famine—a serious shortage of food resulting in widespread hunger and death
refugee—a person forced to flee his or her home country because of war, poverty, natural disaster, or persecution
civil war—a war between opposing groups within one country
culture—a group of people's beliefs, customs, and way of life

CRISIS IN SUDAN

Sudan is a country in Central Africa that has experienced a great deal of war and death. Many people were killed due to their race, **ethnicity**, religion, or political views. Thousands of people have fled to other countries to escape this violence.

From 1955 to 1972, a civil war was fought between the northern and southern parts of Sudan. A second civil war lasted from 1983 to 2005. In 2011 South Sudan officially became an independent country. However, in 2013, a civil war broke out there.

In 2003 a government-backed **militia** began battling with people in the Darfur region of Sudan. The militia tortured people and prevented them from receiving food and medical supplies.

The ongoing violence in Sudan and South Sudan has killed millions of people. Millions more have been forced from their homes. Many people from Sudan, particularly those from Darfur, have resettled in places around the world, including the United States.

Heavily armed members of a militia group patrol the streets in Darfur.

ethnicity—a group of people who share the same language, culture, beliefs, and backgrounds
militia—a group of citizens who are organized to fight but are not professional soldiers

SOMALIA AT WAR

Somalia is a country on the Horn of Africa—a piece of land in northeastern Africa that juts into the Indian Ocean. The capital of Somalia is Mogadishu, a city of more than 2 million people.

Civil war erupted in Somalia in 1991. Different groups fought for power and control of the country. By the end of 1992, 350,000 Somalis had died due to the violence, disease, or starvation. As this civil war went on, more than a million Somalis were left homeless.

The civil war destroyed most of the country's crops. Other countries stepped in to offer food, but often those supplies were stolen by the warring groups. Famine spread throughout the country.

Many Somalis escaped to refugee camps in bordering Kenya. Many of the refugees hoped to return to Somalia, but the conflict has continued for more than two decades. In addition, severe droughts in 2011 and 2017 caused famine throughout Somalia. As a result of the ongoing violence and famine, the refugee camps have become their permanent homes. Refugees often wait months, years, or even decades to resettle in other countries such as the United States. More than 200,000 Somalis currently reside in Dadaab, the largest refugee camp in Kenya.

SOMALIA AND EASTERN AFRICA

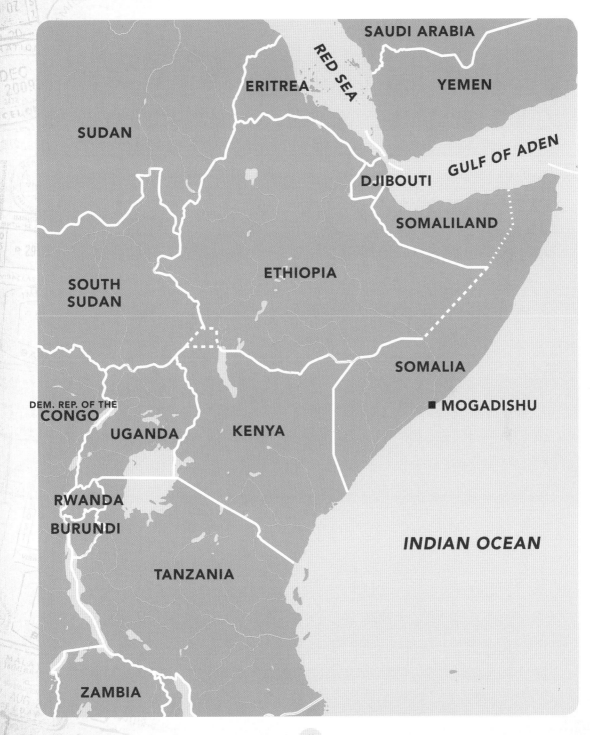

RESETTLING IN A NEW COUNTRY

Those living in refugee camps often wish to resettle in a different country. To do so refugees must apply for resettlement. To resettle in the United States, refugees must be referred by the United Nations High Commissioner for Refugees (UNHCR). The process often takes months or years.

THE DIFFERENCE BETWEEN IMMIGRANTS AND REFUGEES

Immigrants are people who willingly leave their home countries to live someplace else. Refugees have been forced to leave their home countries because of war, famine, or other factors that put them in danger. Many refugees cannot return to their home countries. They fear that, because of their race, religion, or political opinions, returning would put them in danger.

The process for refugees to come to the United States is different than it is for immigrants. Immigrants must be **sponsored** by a U.S. employer or a relative who is a U.S. citizen or permanent resident. They must then apply for an immigrant **visa**. Once they are living in the United States, they may apply for permanent resident or "green card" status. After five years, green card holders can apply to become U.S. citizens.

Refugees need to apply for resettlement. They must go through several steps before being allowed to move to the United States. After living in the United States for a year, refugees can apply for

PROCESS FOR REFUGEES ENTERING THE UNITED STATES

1. A refugee applies for resettlement.

2. The UNHCR decides whether or not the person meets the qualifications for a refugee.

3. A refugee is referred to the United States for resettlement.

4. U.S. law enforcement agencies run background checks on the refugee.

5. Someone from the Department of Homeland Security interviews the refugee.

6. If approved by the Homeland Security officer, the refugee must be checked out by a doctor.

7. The refugee is paired with a partner agency that will help him or her in the United States. Partner agencies include the International Rescue Committee, World Relief, and Lutheran Immigration and Refugee Service.

8. The refugee receives training on how to adapt to American culture. This may include English classes or training on how to use electricity or indoor plumbing.

9. Before leaving for the United States, another background check is completed to look for new information.

10. Once in the United States, airport security people ask the refugee questions. This is to prove that he or she is the same person who was approved as a refugee.

11. The refugee is met by someone from the partner agency he or she was paired with.

sponsor—to be responsible for

visa—a government document that lets the holder enter and leave a foreign country and indicates how long he or she can stay there

A SOMALI IMMIGRANT'S STORY

Deq Ahmed was 5 years old and living in Mogadishu when civil war broke out in Somalia. The day the war erupted, Deq heard bangs and booms in his neighborhood. The Ahmed family fled to the rural areas of Somalia, where they stayed with relatives. Food was so scarce that Deq and his family went days with nothing to eat or drink except camel's milk.

After a few months, the family went back to Mogadishu. Half their house had been blown apart by bombs. Deq heard gunshots day and night. After a few months in Mogadishu, the Ahmed family fled again. This time they were bound for a refugee camp in Kenya.

Like the Ahmed family's home, this house in Mogadishu was blown apart by bombs.

Somali children at a madrassa in a refugee camp practice writing verses from the Koran on planks of wood.

Deq Ahmed and his family left Somalia in 1991 and fled to the refugee camps in Kenya. The family moved back and forth between Mombasa, a city on the Kenyan coast, and the nearby Utange refugee camp. Life in the refugee camp was safer than life in Mogadishu. Deq didn't have to worry about gunfire anymore, but there was little food.

The only school in Utange was a religious school called a *madrassa*. Deq and the other children attended madrassa, where they learned the Koran, the holy book of Islam.

The Ahmed family lived in refugee camps for four years until they were able to resettle in the United States. The Ahmeds were lucky to have family members living in the United States. Deq's uncle had worked for the U.S. government prior to the Somali Civil War. This connection allowed him to move his family to Portland, Oregon. In 1995 Deq's uncle was able to sponsor Deq's family to move to the United States.

Much like the Ahmeds, this family spent years living in a Kenyan refugee camp after fleeing war-torn Somalia. Here, they are arriving in Portland, Oregon, to start their lives in the United States.

Most African immigrants settle in cities when they arrive in the United States. The cities with the highest number of Somali Americans are Minneapolis–St. Paul, Minnesota; Columbus, Ohio; and Seattle, Washington.

An organization known as Lutheran Immigration and Refugee Service helped the Ahmed family on their journey to the United States. When they arrived in New York City in February 1995, Deq and his family saw snow for the first time. The Ahmeds took another plane to their final destination of Portland.

Mariano Mawein moved to the United States from South Sudan.

CHALLENGES AND SUCCESSES

When immigrants arrive in the United States, they face a number of challenges. One of the main challenges is language. Many immigrants from Somalia and other parts of Africa don't speak English. Others may know very little of the language. This language difference can make it difficult for immigrants to get jobs or attend school.

When Deq Ahmed arrived in the United States at age 9, he didn't know English. At first school was very difficult because he didn't know the language. But as he watched American TV shows, he began to learn more English. His school's English Language Learner (ELL) program helped him as well.

Poverty is another challenge immigrants face. They may take low-paying jobs because they don't speak English or lack higher education.

A young girl from Uganda works on a math problem with an ELL teacher in Portland.

Immigrant children in St. Paul work on their English skills with an ELL teacher.

Before the civil war, Deq Ahmed's father worked as an **engineer** in Somalia. The Ahmed family had a comfortable life. But in Portland Deq's father could only find low-paying jobs. His mother had not worked outside the home in Somalia, so she struggled to find a job in Portland.

After about a year in Portland, the family moved to Minneapolis, which had a larger Somali population and more job opportunities. The Ahmed family moved in with friends until they were able to find their own place.

engineer—someone trained to design and build machines, vehicles, bridges, roads, or other structures

PREJUDICE AND DISCRIMINATION

Prejudice is yet another challenge that many immigrants face in the United States. Some Americans fear that immigrants will take jobs away from U.S. citizens. Immigrants also face **discrimination** based on their ethnicity and religious beliefs.

Most immigrants from Somalia are Muslim, which means they follow the religion of Islam. After the terrorist attacks on September 11, 2001, some Americans became prejudiced against Muslims. They feel that all Muslims are against the United States and its beliefs. They fear the Muslim immigrants will launch more terrorist attacks against the United States. Many Muslims still experience this prejudice.

Somali immigrants suffer from these anti-Muslim ideas. Some Somali Americans have been the victims of hate crimes. They have been yelled at, spit on, or physically attacked due to their religious beliefs. Deq Ahmed has been called names due to his race. He's also had people tell him to go back to his Muslim country.

Some Somali businesses have been the target of hate crimes. In 2015 a Somali restaurant in Grand Forks, North Dakota, was spray-painted with the words "Go home." The same restaurant was later set on fire.

Abdulaziz Moallin inspects the damage to his coffee shop in Grand Forks, North Dakota. It was burned during a hate crime.

prejudice—hatred or dislike of people who belong to a certain social group, such as a race or religion
discrimination—treating people unfairly because of their race, country of birth, or gender

SUCCESSFUL COMMUNITIES

Despite the challenges, Somali immigrants often find success and happiness in the United States. Somalis often settle in communities with other Somali immigrants. Within these close-knit communities, immigrants provide support and help for each other. When Deq Ahmed and his family moved to Minneapolis, he had several Somali classmates in his fifth-grade classroom. Deq was happy to have fellow Somalis in his class.

THE PATH TO CITIZENSHIP

Many refugees and immigrants hope to become U.S. citizens, but there are many steps in this process. First, refugees and immigrants who wish to become citizens must be green card holders for five years. Adults age 18 or older may then apply for citizenship. They must fill out forms, pay processing fees, and go through an interview. They must also pass an English test and a test on U.S. government and history. The final step is to take an oath of **allegiance** to the United States

Many cities offer support for immigrants, such as the Confederation of Somali Community in Minnesota and the Somali Community Association of Ohio. These organizations provide resources

A Somali business owner stocks the shelves of her grocery store in Maine.

to help Somali immigrants adjust to life in the United States while still maintaining their culture.

Some Somali immigrants open their own businesses, such as grocery stores, restaurants, and clothing stores. These businesses help build Somali American communities. Somali businesses help new immigrants from Somalia feel at home and help long-term immigrants maintain their culture. These businesses also allow other Americans to explore Somali culture, food, and customs.

allegiance—loyalty and obedience owed to one's country or government

LOOKING TO THE FUTURE

Immigration laws in the United States are ever-changing. Laws have been put in place to stop illegal immigration. Illegal immigration means moving to a country without the government's permission or official documentation. Other laws limit the number of immigrants and refugees. The Immigration Act of 1990 said that 675,000 immigrants could move to the United States each year. Every year the U.S. president determines the number of refugees who can be admitted into the country. In 2016 President Barack Obama said 110,000 refugees could come to the United States the following year. President Donald Trump lowered the number to 45,000 for 2018.

In 2017 President Trump also issued an **executive order** that limited or banned travel and immigration from eight countries. According to Trump, the purpose of these limits is to protect the United States from **terrorism**. Because a terrorist group is active in Somalia, the country was included on the list. Depending on the traveler's immigration status, some travel to and from Somalia is allowed. However, the executive order banned all further immigration from Somalia.

The unrest in Somalia has lasted many years. A central government is in place, but the nation still faces issues with terrorism. A terrorist group controls parts of the country. In October 2017 a terrorist attack in Mogadishu killed more than 300 Somalis.

On January 29, 2017, Americans protested President Trump's executive order banning people from several Muslim countries from entering the United States.

executive order—an order that comes from the U.S. president or a government agency and must be obeyed like a law

terrorism—the use of violence and destructive acts to create fear and achieve political or religious goals

Many Somali Americans were upset by the executive order. Some were hoping that family members in Somalia would be able to move to the United States. Others felt that Somalis were suffering due to the actions of terrorist groups.

★ THE FUTURE OF SOMALI AMERICANS ★

Deq Ahmed now has a college degree and has worked as a librarian and teacher. As an immigrant himself, he understands the challenges Somali youth face. As a teacher he helped Somali students and their families adapt to American culture. "We're trying to find ways to help families and . . . students fit into the society that they live in," he said. "You are an American first, Somali second."

Deq would like to see Somali Americans and other Americans learn about each other's cultures. For example, he believes Christians should learn about Islam, and Muslims should learn about Christianity. "I am a Muslim," he said, "but I want to know what other people believe and how they think compared to how I'm thinking. It only helps me grow as a person." Deq believes this would help bring an end to prejudice based on religious beliefs.

TOP COUNTRIES OF ORIGIN FOR AFRICAN IMMIGRANTS IN THE UNITED STATES AS OF 2016

CAPE VERDE
45,000

SIERRA LEONE
38,000

LIBERIA
88,000

GHANA
171,000

NIGERIA
307,000

CAMEROON
49,000

SUDAN
39,000

ERITREA
43,000

ETHIOPIA
245,000

SOMALIA
93,000

KENYA
130,000

SOUTH AFRICA
105,000

Source: Migration Policy Institute

Deq has witnessed some of the positive steps Somali Americans have taken to improve their lives. Many have become leaders at the local, state, and national levels. In 2010 Hussein Samatar won a seat on the Minneapolis school board. Abdi Warsame was elected to the Minneapolis City Council in 2013. They are among the first Somali Americans to serve in public office. In 2017 four Somali Americans won local elections around the country. Somali Americans are hopeful for the future as they continue embracing their religion and culture, all while pursuing the American dream.

Minneapolis City Council member Abdi Warsame (left) speaks to the community.

ILHAN OMAR

In 2016 Ilhan Omar became the first Somali American Muslim elected to a state legislature. Ilhan and her family fled the Somali Civil War in 1991 when she was 8 years old. Her family lived in the Utange refugee camp in Kenya for four years before resettling in the United States. They lived in Arlington, Virginia, before moving to Minneapolis.

As a child, Ilhan first became interested in politics after attending a political meeting with her grandfather. In 2016 she was elected to the Minnesota House of Representatives.

GLOSSARY

allegiance (uh-LEE-juhnts)—loyalty and obedience owed to one's country or government

civil war (SIV-il WOR)—a war between opposing groups within one country

culture (KUHL-chur)—a group of people's beliefs, customs, and way of life

discrimination (dis-kri-muh-NAY-shuhn)—treating people unfairly because of their race, country of birth, or gender

drought (DROUT)—a long period of weather with little or no rainfall

engineer (en-juh-NEER)—someone trained to design and build machines, vehicles, bridges, roads, or other structures

ethnicity (eth-NI-sit-ee)—a group of people who share the same language, culture, beliefs, and backgrounds

executive order (ig-ZEK-yuh-tiv OR-dur)—an order that comes from the U.S. president or a government agency and must be obeyed like a law

famine (FA-muhn)—a serious shortage of food resulting in widespread hunger and death

immigrant (IM-uh-gruhnt)—someone who comes from one country to live permanently in another country

militia (muh-LISH-uh)—a group of citizens who are organized to fight but are not professional soldiers

prejudice (PREJ-uh-diss)—hatred or dislike of people who belong to a certain social group, such as a race or religion

refugee (ref-yuh-JEE)—a person forced to flee his or her home country because of war, poverty, natural disaster, or persecution

sponsor (SPAHN-sur)—to be responsible for

terrorism (TER-ur-i-zuhm)—the use of violence and destructive acts to create fear and achieve political or religious goals

visa (VEE-zuh)—a government document that lets the holder enter and leave a foreign country and indicates how long he or she can stay there

READ MORE

Creager, Ellen. *Life as a Somali American.* One Nation for All: Immigrants in the United States. New York, PowerKids Press, 2018.

Glynne, Andy. *Hamid's Story: A Real-Life Account of His Journey from Eritrea.* Seeking Refuge. North Mankato, Minn.: Picture Window Books, 2018.

Rodger, Ellen. *A Refugee's Journey from South Sudan.* Leaving My Homeland. New York: Crabtree Publishing, 2018.

INTERNET SITES

Use FactHound to find Internet sites related to this book.

Visit www.facthound.com

Just type in 9781543513813 and go.

 Check out projects, games and lots more at
www.capstonekids.com

CRITICAL THINKING QUESTIONS

1. Describe the challenges faced by immigrants from Africa. Do you think immigrants from other parts of the world experience the same challenges? Why or why not? Use evidence from the text and your own knowledge to support your answers.

2. Study the infographic on page 5. Why do you think immigration from African nations has increased so much since 1970? Use evidence from the text to support your answer.

3. Describe reasons refugees from Somalia or the Sudan might choose to resettle in the United States. Give reasons for your answer based on the text and your own thinking.

INDEX

31901063419875